BUILDING AMERICA

THE FARMS

BUILDING AMERICA

THE FARMS

Raymond Bial

BENCHMARK BOOKS
MARSHALL CAVENDISH
NEW YORK

This book is dedicated to America's farm families,
who put in long hours on the land.

Benchmark Books
Marshall Cavendish
99 White Plains Road
Tarrytown, New York 10591-9001
Website: www.marshallcavendish.com

Library of Congress Cataloging-in-Publication Data
Bial, Raymond.
    The Farms / by Raymond Bial.
        p. cm. – (Building America)
    Includes bibliographical references and index.
    ISBN 0-7614-1332-4
        1. Agriculture—United States—History—Juvenile literature. 2. Farms, Small—United States—History—Juvenile literature. [1. Farms—History. 2. Agriculture—History.] I. Title.
S519 .B528 2001   630'.973—dc21   00-065071

Printed in Hong Kong
6 5 4 3 2 1

Cover Photo: Raymond Bial

The photographs in this book are used by permission through the courtesy of: *North Wind Pictures*: 6, 8, 30. *Corbis*: 13, 25, 26. *Raymond Bial*: 14, 16, 18, 22, 38, 45, 47, 48, back cover. *Unicorn Stock Photos*: Frank Pennington: 46. *The Eric Sloane Estate*: 21, 29, 33, 36, 37, 40, 41, 43, 44.

Book design by Clair Moritz-Magnesio

CONTENTS

Many people came to America in hopes of clearing a few acres of land and making a home for their families.

Introduction

"The history of a people is inseparable from the country it inhabits."
—Fernand Braudel

Most settlers who journeyed to North America and then ventured westward were farmers. They shared a common dream of clearing a few acres, building a house and a barn, and living off the land. In Europe, only a few people belonged to the upper class, while all the rest were of the lower class. These masses had little control over their destinies. Often, they were not allowed to follow their own religious beliefs. Or they were forced to become soldiers in the king's army. Most had no hope of owning a farm. However, if they sailed across the Atlantic Ocean, they had a chance to pursue free and independent lives. They certainly faced many hardships and dangers as they ventured into a strange new world, but land was plentiful and cheap. For example, a German immigrant could buy one hundred acres of fertile ground in Pennsylvania for the same cost as the rent on the same amount of land in Europe for one year. Others, such as inden-

Brought to North America against their will, slaves, and their descendants, worked the plantations of the South.

tured servants and slaves, came to North America in bondage. Yet they, too, often hoped to someday own a farm on which they would serve no master.

In early colonial years, several European nations—Britain, France, Spain, and Holland—gave huge tracts of land to wealthy and influential people to encourage settlement in North America. These grantees then sold off sections of their holdings to the new colonists. The single house on a plot of land became the common pattern in America, especially in the British colonies along the Atlantic coast. Family life revolved around the farm, with the husband, wife, and children all working the land. Colonial farmers learned how to plant corn, squash, and other crops from Native Americans who had farmed the land for hundreds of years. Over time, hardy pioneers made their way over the Appalachian Mountains and made their homes in the hills of Kentucky. Others moved into the woodlands of Ohio and Indiana, while the French claimed the Mississippi Valley, from the bayous of Louisiana to Illinois Country.

Large plantations developed in the Chesapeake Bay region and gradually spread throughout the South, and Spanish colonists had already established sprawling estates known as *ranchos* in the Southwest. Most of the labor on these estates was undertaken by people forced to work against their will. However, by the late seventeenth century, the family homestead on which people lived freely on their own land became firmly established across North America, from Maine to Oregon. These small farms relied on many kinds of buildings and other structures for housing livestock, undertaking daily work, and storing feed and crops.

Spring on a farm meant hard work—it was time to clear another field and prepare the soil for planting.

1

HOMESTEADING

After the Revolutionary War, the United States awarded land grants to the veterans, who rushed as far west as the Mississippi River to claim their lands. Others sold their land to speculators, giving up the chance of having their own farms. Some pioneers simply squatted on a plot of land, marked off their own boundaries, and set to work. But overlapping claims often led to disputes. Such a dispute forced Abraham Lincoln's father, Thomas Lincoln, to move his family from Kentucky to Indiana. Others viewed farm life simply as a means of eking out a living. After homesteader Howard Ruede moved to the Allegheny foothills of Pennsylvania, his aunt praised his courage. He said to his mother, "She makes me out to be a hero, but for the life of me I can't see anything heroic in coming out here to do farm work." Yet leaders such as Thomas Jefferson believed that democracy would not succeed unless the United States became a nation of small farmers.

Throughout the nineteenth century, settlers moved west to claim land for farming, ranching, and mining. Many families chose to homestead beneath the open skies of the Great Plains, which sprawled from North Dakota to Texas and from the Mississippi River to the Rocky Mountains. After winning its independence from Mexico in 1836, the Republic of Texas awarded land to the soldiers who had fought in the revolution. In the Mexican War of 1846–1848, the United States seized the remainder of the Southwest from Mexico. Settlers claimed thousands of acres for farms and ranches in the region that eventually became the states of New Mexico, Arizona, and California.

President Abraham Lincoln signed the Homestead Act of 1862 to encourage settlement of the West, especially of the Great Plains. Settlers received 160-acre parcels, which they would own if they lived on the land for five years. People took advantage of the Homestead Act to stake their claim. A popular song captured the sense of promise in the air:

O come to this country,
And don't you feel alarm
For Uncle Sam is rich enough
To give us all a farm

Yet homesteading was not to be undertaken lightly. No matter where they farmed, homesteaders had to provide for the daily needs of their families and to prepare for the future. As Percy Ebbutt, an English immigrant to Kansas, wrote in a guide for pioneers:

> *You must make up your mind to rough it. You must cultivate the habit of sleeping in any kind of surroundings, on a board and without*

Swinging sharp-bladed axes, pioneers chopped down trees and trimmed the branches from the trunks. They used the logs to build cabins.

a pillow, indoors or out.

You must be prepared to cook your own dinner, darn your own socks if you wear them, and think yourself fortunate if you are not reduced to the position of a man I knew, who lay in a bed while his wife mended his only pair of trousers.

Learn to ride as soon as you possibly can; a man or boy who cannot ride is, in a new country, about as valuable as a clerk who cannot write in a city office.

In the latter half of the nineteenth century, thousands of pioneers journeyed by covered wagon to California and Oregon. In agreeing to marry Fails Howard in the Willamette valley of Oregon, Parmelia Greenstreet declared, "Sure, I'll marry you: a farm like that looks good to me and so do you." Less than three centuries after the first colonists had landed on the coast of the Atlantic Ocean, the frontier had shifted across the continent to the shores of the Pacific. John Floyd, a political leader from Virginia expressed the pride of many: "With two great oceans washing our shores, commercial wealth is ours and imagination can hardly conceive the greatness, the grandeur, the power that await us."

Settlers established many kinds of farms in the hills and the valleys of the American frontier, from New England to Kentucky.

2

FARMING THE LAND

Settlers brought their skills and knowledge from the home country. There were German, Scotch-Irish, and English immigrants, as well as Americans whose families had lived on this continent for generations. New England Yankees and Virginians moved into Kentucky. Scandinavians, Finns, Russians, and Eastern European immigrants went to Wisconsin, Minnesota, and the Dakotas; Spanish-Americans lived in the Southwest. Cajuns and other people of French descent made their homes in Louisiana and spread north along the muddy course of the Mississippi River. Each group brought its own cultural heritage and ways of farming the land.

Farms were shaped by the climate and the terrain in which they were found—in hills or valleys, along rivers or on floodplains, in the desert or on the prairie. And beneath it all lay the soil. One man described the Great Plains as ". . . like an ocean in its vast extent, in its monotony, and in its danger." Yet farmers turned this flat and fertile land

Early homesteaders often constructed sturdy log barns to shelter their livestock and to store hay, corn, and other feed.

into fields of corn, wheat, and other valuable crops and planted vegetable gardens near their houses. They often used hilly land, which could not be easily plowed, as pasture for cattle and sheep. Homesteaders prospered in some regions, while others faced hardship. One pioneer in Council Grove, Kansas, complained, "Between the drought, the cinch bugs, and grasshoppers, we will be forced to go to Egypt or somewhere else for our corn." But another young pioneer wrote of Nebraska to his mother back east, "Ma, you can see as far as you please here and almost every foot in sight can be plowed." Similarly, in Oregon Territory, the "genial soil," as one farmer put it, proved excellent. The fertile yet affordable farmland of Oregon was considered "the best poor man's country on the globe."

A small family homestead usually included a field and a garden plot, along with a milk cow, a flock of chickens, a herd of sheep, and a few hogs rooting for acorns in the nearby woods. Homesteaders often had a team of oxen or draft horses for working their farms. There were also cattle ranches and dairy farms and many farms that evolved into growing a single crop such as tobacco, cotton, or wheat.

Split-rail fences were built from the hills of Virginia to the prairies of Illinois.

3

ROADS AND FENCES

A farm had to be located near a road, whether it was a pair of ruts winding through the woods or a well-traveled thoroughfare, so that wagons and buggies could be driven to market in a nearby village. A lane led to the house and the farmyard where the barn and outbuildings stood. The boundaries of the farm were marked by stone walls or split-rail fences. Throughout the East, farmers picked stones from their fields and piled them into walls that staunchly withstood the weather—be it heaving frost, baking sun, or drenching rain. In

New England, these low walls still wind over hills and valleys.

In Europe, wood was scarce and there were not many fences. However, from the vast forests of North America—especially if there were no stones to be cleared from fields—homesteaders built sturdy wooden fences, many of which have lasted for generations. These fences protected crops from hungry animals, including their own hogs and chickens. Often, the livestock freely roamed the farm and were fenced *out* of the garden and fields. The several types of wood fences included the New England cross-and-rail in which four rails were laid between two crossed posts, two above and two below the cross. There was also the Virginia stake-and-rail fence in which rails were stacked between pairs of fence posts. In Ohio and elsewhere in the Midwest, some farmers built post-and-rail fences in which the ends of the rails were placed in notches bored and chiseled in the posts.

However, the most common fence on pioneer homesteads was the Virginia snake fence, or split-rail fence. This fence consisted of rails stacked in a zigzag pattern and did not require any nails. With steel wedges and hammers, men split long, straight logs of oak, cedar, ash, or chestnut into quarters or eighths. These became the rails. Split-rail fences required enormous amounts of wood—one acre of forest for every ten acres enclosed. Some settlers also constructed board fences thickly lined with brush in an effort to keep rabbits and other small animals out of the garden. However, nothing could keep white-tailed deer from springing over the fence and nibbling young sprouts. So, ripening crops still had to be vigilantly watched.

After barbed wire was patented in 1874, ranchers fenced off land from the Mississippi River to the Rocky Mountains. Over time, many switched from cattle ranching to grain farming. Rolling fields of wheat stretched over the Great Plains. People also homesteaded in Montana, where they endured bitterly cold winters, and in the deserts of New Mexico and Arizona, where they faced intense summer heat.

FENCE *building was an American Art.*

2 ABOVE, 2 BELOW

New England Cross-and-Rail C...*with stones added*

Vermont

Virginia Stake-and-rail

Snake

Straight

Virginia Snake fence

Bored
or
Chiselled

POST
and
RAIL

Ohio

These drawings by Eric Sloane illustrate the most common types of fences erected on homesteads where wood was abundant.

With its tin roof rusting and its boards fading in the weather, this old barn in the Appalachian Mountains stands as a reminder of better days.

4

EARLY BARNS

Besides the house, farms had many buildings. The largest and most important of these was the barn. Often more than sixty feet long, thirty feet wide, and sixteen feet high, the barn sheltered cattle, horses, and other livestock. Homesteaders also stored hay, corn, and grain in their barns. Farmers constructed many kinds of barns that have endured for centuries. In 1790, Isaac Weld, an Irish visitor, said of the early farmers, "These people are so certain of their futures that they spend a lifetime building homes for future generations."

Barns varied among ethnic groups and regions. Building materials might be hewn logs or sawn boards, but the structures were functionally the same.

The first barns of North America were made of rough hewn and crudely notched logs, coarse wooden shingles, and handwrought hardware, that is, if the doors even had latches and hinges. Neighbors often came together in work parties, which were called frolics or bees, to construct log barns. These included log rollings and barn raisings and usually took place when a new family arrived to homestead or a couple married.

Early in the morning, people arrived who had walked or ridden horses from as far as ten miles away. Sandford C. Cox, a pioneer living along the Wabash River in the early 1800s, noted that he and his neighbors had "cleared lands, rolled logs, and burned brush, blazed out paths from one cabin to another." In a single day of log rolling, a group of ax-swinging men could clear five to eight acres of land. Women and children wielded small axes or sharp-bladed tools called bushwhacks to clear away brush, which they then piled and burned. Using teams of oxen or horses, the men either pulled out the stumps that remained stubbornly rooted in the soil or they planted around them.

In a barn raising, men hewed the logs into square timbers for the frame, if the settler had not yet done this work. In *Home Life in Early Indiana*, William F. Vogel wrote, "The neighbors divided themselves into choppers, hewers, carpenters, and masons. Those who found it impossible to report for duty might pay an equivalent in nails, boards, or other materials." Homesteaders laid out a stone foundation. Groups of men fitted the timbers together to form the walls and then lifted the heavy rafters of the roof into place. They sheathed the roof with hand-riven shingles, thatch, or sod.

People have gathered with wagon loads of supplies in about 1900, ready to work on a farm in Minnesota. Without help from neighbors, many farmers would not have prospered.

Entitled "He That Tilleth the Land is Satisfied," this 1850 painting of a Pennsylvania farm portrays an idyllic life on the land.

5

ENGLISH AND DUTCH BARNS

The first post-and-beam barns in North America were built by English and Dutch settlers in New England. In these barns, the posts and the beams, or the vertical and horizontal timbers, formed the structure of the walls. To prepare the timbers, people skillfully squared them with broadaxes and adzes. With handsaws and chisels, they cut mortise-and-tenon joints at the ends of the timbers. (A projecting part in one timber fit into a slot in another one.) With augers, builders drilled holes in the notches of the joints so wooden pegs called treenails (TRUHN-nels) could be driven through to secure the joints. They next laid the posts and beams out on the ground together to make the walls. Matching the joints and holes, they drove in the treenails. Now they were ready to raise the sturdy walls. To fill the spaces of the walls, men sided the barn with lumber, such as clapboard, board and batten, or tongue-and-groove siding. To build the roof, they cut timbers for the rafters, pegged them together, and covered them with shingles.

The double doors of English barns typically opened onto a threshing floor, and livestock pens ran along the sides. Styles of English barns remained popular through the nineteenth century, when many were built in the Midwest and on the Canadian plains.

Although not as widespread as English barns, the Dutch built many barns in the Hudson, Mohawk, and Schoharie Valleys in what is now New York State, as well as in neighboring New Jersey. These barns had wide gable roofs that reached low to the ground and were tall enough to hold huge amounts of hay. The only openings in the massive walls other than the wide doors for wagons were small holes for the martins that made their nests inside. These birds were welcomed on farms because they devoured large numbers of the insects that damaged crops.

Dutch barns were made of heavy beams, which were mortised, tenoned, and pegged to form H-shaped frames. The timbers stood like columns along the aisles on either side of the barn. The wood siding was usually laid horizontally. Most Dutch barns are gone now, although a few from the late eighteenth century remain standing—a testament to the pride and skill of those who built them.

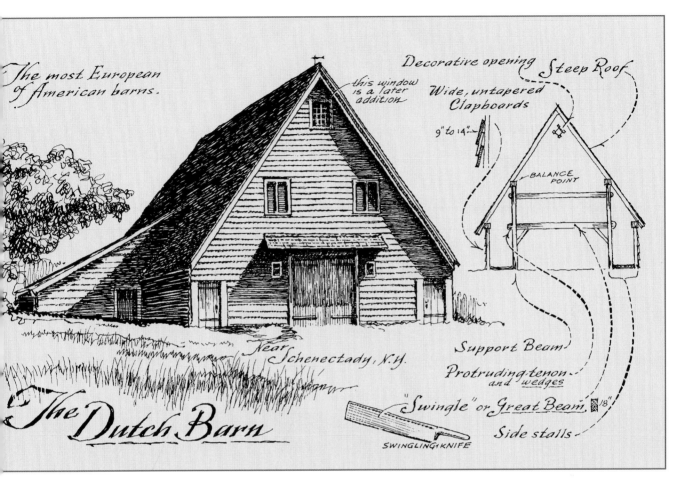

The most European of American barns.

this window is a later addition

Decorative opening

Steep Roof

Wide, untapered Clapboards

9" to 14"

BALANCE POINT

Near Schenectady, N.Y.

The Dutch Barn

Support Beam

Protruding tenon and wedges

"Swingle" or Great Beam 18"

Side stalls

SWINGLING KNIFE

This Dutch barn features an H-shaped beam structure on the inside and a low-sloping roof that nearly reaches the ground.

This barn, built by Shakers in New Hampshire, is an example of a Pennsylvania, or bank, barn.

6

PENNSYLVANNIA BARNS

The *American Agriculturist* magazine wrote: "An ample barn for the storage of crops and the shelter of stock should be regarded as a necessary investment of capital in all farming in the Northern and Eastern States. This is better understood in Pennsylvania than in any other part of the country, and the barn that bears the name of the State is, in many respects, a model." The Pennsylvania barn was also known as a bank barn or sidehill barn, so named because it was built into the slope of a hill. The lower level housed live-stock, and the upper level was used as a threshing floor and storage place. The hillside entrance allowed wagons of wheat or hay to be pulled inside to either the upper or lower level. Fodder, or feed, was dropped through openings in the second floor to the stalls below where the live-stock were stabled. If the farm did not have a hill, a ramp to the second floor might be built by fashioning an earthen bank.

The long side of the bank barn ran parallel to the hill, usually on its south side so livestock could gather there in the warmth of the sun during the winter. To provide even more shelter, the second floor was cantilevered, or extended, at least six feet beyond the foundation to make a forebay, or overhang. If the beams were not large enough to bear the weight from above, posts were placed beneath the forebay for sup-port. In the earliest Pennsylvania barns, the walls of the narrow ends were frequently made of stone or brick. There were openings in the walls that offered ventilation. This was crucial because when green hay dried out it could give off enough heat to burst into flame.

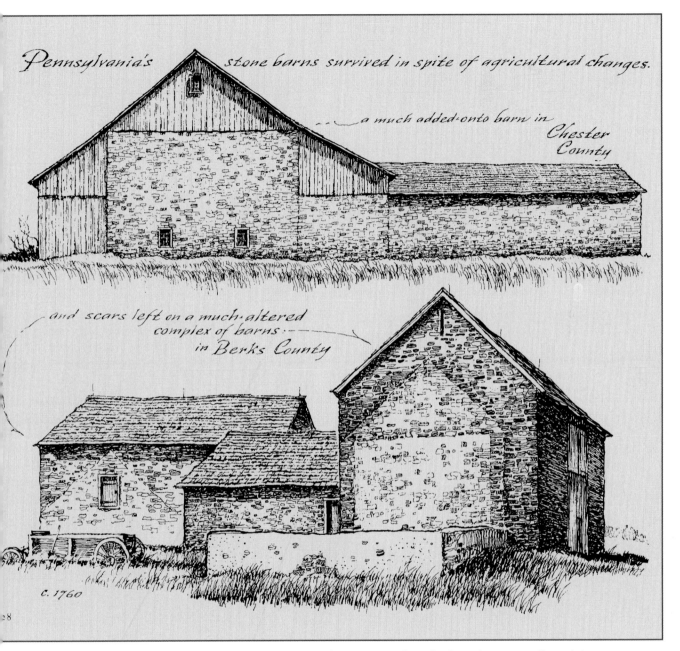

Pennsylvania's stone barns survived in spite of agricultural changes.

...a much added-onto barn in Chester County

and scars left on a much-altered complex of barns:— in Berks County

c. 1760

28

Among the most impressive barns in Pennsylvania were those built with stones collected from the fields.

Gambrel barns, such as this one in Minnesota, blended elements of Dutch, English, and Pennsylvania styles. Often painted "barn red" and trimmed in white, they came to symbolize the American farmer.

7

CRIB BARNS, PRAIRIE BARNS, AND MORE

Many other kinds of barns were scattered across America. Farmers built crib barns, especially in the Appalachian and Ozark Mountains of North Carolina, Virginia, Kentucky, Tennessee, and Arkansas. These were simple structures, with one to six cribs, or rooms, for storing fodder or sheltering cattle and pigs and perhaps a haymow above the ground floor. Most early crib barns had roofs made of shingles. Crib barns were usually built of unchinked logs, although sometimes the spaces between the timbers were chinked with mud or clay or sheethed with wooden siding. If well chinked, timber barns were quite warm. With their thick walls, they resisted fire better and lasted longer than timber-frame barns covered with sawn boards.

In the West, ranchers put up enormous prairie barns for storing the huge amounts of hay needed to feed their herds of cattle through the long, cold winter months. These barns had broad roofs that jutted out over the hayloft door and nearly reached the ground. By the late 1800s these barns were more often built with gambrel roofs, having a double-slope on each side. The gambrel roof increased the storage space within the haymow. Prairie barns were very similar to traditional Dutch barns:

Homesteaders relied on many kinds of outbuildings, including corn cribs, sheds, and barns, made from rough-hewn logs.

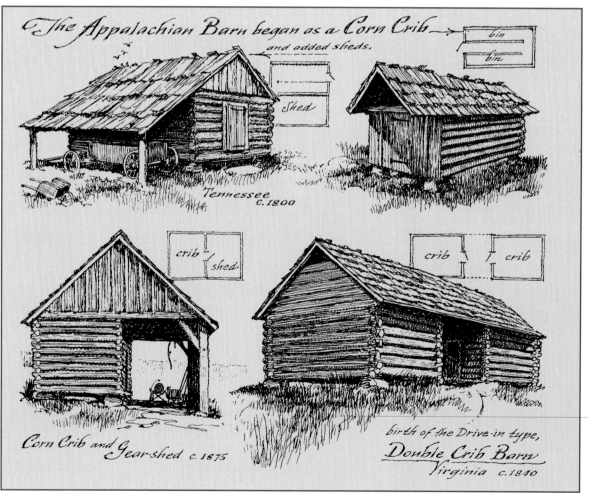

The Appalachian Barn began as a Corn Crib and added sheds.

bin

bin

shed

Tennessee c. 1800

crib / shed

crib / crib

Corn Crib and Gear-shed c. 1875

birth of the Drive-in type,
Double Crib Barn
Virginia c. 1840

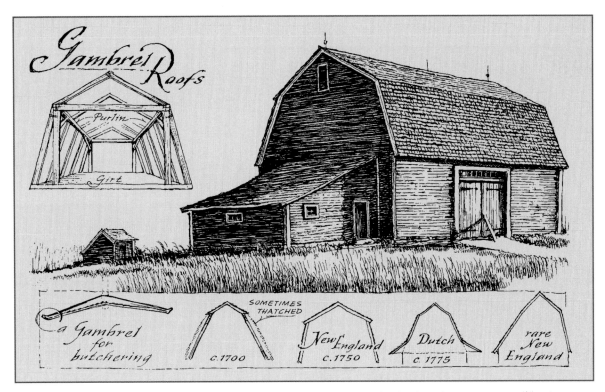

The gambrel roof, which provided spacious storage room in the hayloft, became a common feature of many kinds of barns.

they had a low, sweeping roof, a door in the gable side, and stalls lining either side of the interior.

Immigrants built their own distinctive barns: Finnish log barns went up in Idaho and Czech and German-Russian house barns in South Dakota. Other barns were distinguished by their unique building materials—basalt or lava rock in Idaho, logs in southern Appalachia, and adobe in the Southwest. On the prairie, homesteaders, including a number of African-Americans, used the soil itself to make sod barns—as well as sod schools, sod churches, and even a sod post office and a sod hotel. The design of many barns was defined by their use. There were dairy barns for milking cows in the Midwest and barns for drying tobacco in the East and South, large barns for drying hops in the Northwest, and barns for storing rice in South Carolina. Some quirky barns did not fit into any particular style, but were constructed according to the whim and means of the farmer.

Adapted from Native American storage bins, the corn crib, though modest in size, was one of the most important buildings on the farm.

8

OUTBUILDINGS

The barn loomed over the farmyard. Clustered around it were many outbuildings that provided additional space for animals, feed, and equipment. Horses and cows were usually housed in the barn, with adjoining pens or corrals, while hogs and sheep were kept in sheds. Most homesteads had a chicken coop near either the house or the barn—depending on whether the wife or the husband looked after the poultry. Chickens needed good light, warmth, and ventilation, so most coops had large, south-facing windows. As farmers acquired more equipment, they added storage and repair buildings. Sometimes, they built sheds two stories high so loaded hay wagons could be pulled inside. Plantations and large, prosperous farms had carriage houses for protecting horse-drawn vehicles from the weather.

Homesteaders also needed buildings for storing feed. They put up corn cribs adapted from Native American storage huts. Corn cribs always had spaces between the slats to provide good ventilation, and their sides were often wider at the top than at the bottom. The overhang offered protection from the rain. Cribs were raised off the damp ground on stone foundations to keep the corn dry and to protect the hard, yellow grain from hungry mice and rats. Wheat and other grain were sometimes kept in rectangular sheds known as granaries.

This illustration depicts a variety of early corn cribs. All have sloping sides to shed the rain and are raised from the ground to deter mice and rats.

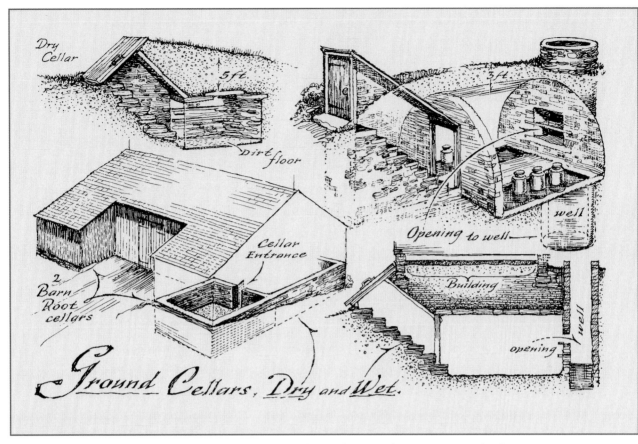

Dry Cellar

5 ft

Dirt floor

Cellar Entrance

2. Barn Root cellars

Opening to well

well

Building

well

opening

Ground Cellars, Dry and Wet.

These drawings show several types of root cellars where apples, potatoes, and other foods were stored.

In the latter half of the nineteenth century, farmers began to keep more livestock. This meant they needed to store large amounts of winter feed—chopped stalks and leaves of green corn. So, they built storage bins called silos. The first silos were stone-lined pits, occasionally dug right inside the barn. Farmers then tried vertical, rectangular silos, but air became trapped in the corners, and the feed spoiled. By the 1880s, farmers were building round silos of wooden staves held together with wire hoops. Concrete silos were not used until well into the twentieth century. After World War II, glass and steel silos, such as those manufactured by Harvestore, were a common sight.

Other buildings essential to daily life were scattered around the farmyard—the springhouse, icehouse, milk house, woodshed, and outhouse. Most farms also had a root cellar, smokehouse, and perhaps a butchering shed. In the fall, potatoes, carrots, apples, and garden produce were stored in layers of sand, sawdust, or hay in cellars. (The word "cellar" comes from a French word meaning "pantry," or storage place for food.) Most root cellars were simply holes dug with a pick and shovel into a slope, but some were elaborate, rock-lined caves with arched entrances. On the Great Plains, dugouts and soddies might be turned into root cellars when settlers were able to move from them into new wood-frame houses. If attacked by Native Americans, settlers occasionally hid in their root cellars. On the prairie, people also took shelter in root cellars when thunderstorms and tornadoes swept over the land.

Settlers knew the value of the cool and constant temperatures in their root cellars. Thick earthen walls provided a frost-proof place for storing vegetables. Root cellars were later dug underneath houses, and furnaces were put inside them. Today, belongings are also stored in basements, but originally women used cellars only to store the foods that the family needed to survive the long winter. Whether the root cellar was dug in the yard or under the house, the slanted outside doorway was designed so a wheelbarrow loaded with produce could be easily steered down a ramp into the cellar. Children also enjoyed sliding down the icy sloping doors during the winter.

In the days before grocery stores and electricity were common, farmers butchered their own hogs, as well as wild game, in sheds fitted with hooks for hanging meat. Next to the butchering shed, they built a smokehouse of brick, stone, or, most often, wood. The smokehouse had to be draft free, so they caulked the boards tightly. Using hickory chips, fruitwood, or corncobs, which nicely flavored the meat, they started a small fire in a pit in the earthen floor. Smoke soon filled the nearly airtight room, blackening the inside walls and preserving the hams and other cuts of meat hanging inside. Farmers usually locked their smokehouses, because cured hams and sides of bacon might attract hungry thieves.

Before refrigeration, most American farms had a small stone or wood-frame smokehouse where hams and bacon were smoked to preserve the meat.

If the homestead had a spring or little stream, a springhouse was built over it. The fresh, burbling waters kept the inside temperatures a nice, cool 50 degrees Fahrenheit. Usually made of stone or brick since wood soon rotted in the damp atmosphere, springhouses were most often built on farms settled in the early 1800s east of the Mississippi River. Farmers used these sturdy little buildings as a cooler for milk, butter, and other perishable foods in the days before refrigeration. Farmers placed crocks of milk in the channels of cold, clear water that ran between the floorboards. Sometimes, springhouses were big enough that people could churn butter in the cool interior.

If the farm lacked a good spring or stream, settlers dug a well by hand. They might then build a well house or pump house to shield the opening. Wells were a source of drinking water, and milk was also kept fresh by lowering it into the cool depths in a bucket. On the prairies, where water was scarce, wind provided an abundant and handy source of energy. People said, "Between Amarillo and the North Pole, there is nothing to stop the wind but a barbed wire fence." So, homesteaders constructed windmills to pump water from deep wells. Stark against the broad skies, these stiltlike wooden structures towered over sod houses and barns as a symbol of the pioneers' triumph over the demands of life on the Great Plains.

In 1854, a mechanic named Daniel Halladay designed the first

Built over a stream or a spring, a springhouse used the running water to keep milk, cream, and other perishables cool during the summer.

This stone springhouse was constructed directly over a small stream whose water flowed through the floor of the building.

windmill that turned so the wooden blades faced the wind. The whirling blades turned a crankshaft that worked the pump up and down. On a typical day, the windmill could draw hundreds of gallons of water from the earth. These large amounts were needed to water cattle and irrigate crops on the parched grasslands.

In the days before electricity, people needed ice not only to chill drinks but to store food. In the northern parts of the country, farmers harvested ice from ponds or rivers during the winter and hauled the blocks to their farms where they stored them in the icehouse. The ice-house rested on a stone foundation and had double wooden walls about six inches apart. The space was packed with sawdust, hay, or leaves. Often partly underground, icehouses were so well insulated that they

Used to pump water from hand-dug wells, windmills became familiar landmarks on many farms from Ohio to Oregon.

could keep ice through the hot summer months. Farmers dug a storage chamber under the floor for fruits and dairy products, especially if they did not have a springhouse. By the 1870s, refrigerated railroad cars brought blocks of ice to many rural communities, and icehouses were a thing of the past.

Over time, farms might also add a blacksmith shop, toolshed, sheep pen, dovecote, washhouse, or perhaps an outdoor kitchen for cooking meals in the heat of the summer. These buildings seemed placed at random around a homestead, except in Maine, New Hampshire, and a few other places where farm buildings were often joined, sometimes even to the house. This allowed the farmer and his family to care for the livestock more easily during winters of deep snow.

Early farmsteads did not have indoor plumbing. Instead there were outhouses, or privies. Usually small, simple buildings made of wood, outhouses did vary in size and might be made of stone or brick. A half-moon on the door indicated a privy for girls and women, because the moon was considered female. A sun, regarded as male, was carved on the door of an outhouse for boys and men. Eventually the half-moon came to indicate all privies. Curiously, archaeologists digging at the sites of old privies often find wonderful treasures—old glass bottles, china, porcelain dolls, and other objects that now have great value—that were discarded in the privy years ago.

With a half-moon carved into the door, the outhouse was considered an essential building in the days before indoor plumbing.

Since modern machinery and methods of farming have taken hold, traditional barns and other out-buildings no longer play an important role. Yet they remain a powerful symbol of a way of life gone by.

9

A RURAL PAST

Mark Twain, who spent portions of his childhood in the country, humorously described a farm as "a creek for swimming, a barn for sleeping, outbuildings for exploration, and a hayloft for relaxing." In truth, to be successful, farms required backbreaking labor. Families were able to provide for themselves on their homesteads only by working together. It was a hard life, but one that tended to bring out the best in people. As one pioneer wrote, "I never saw so fine a population as in Oregon. They were honest, because there was nothing to steal; sober, because there was no liquor; there were no misers because there was no money; they were industrial, because it was work or starve."

Much of America was built on the backs of farmers, who put up the buildings they needed to raise livestock and store the harvest. As farms became more mechanized and modernized in the early 1900s, most of these traditional structures became unnecessary. Today, grain farmers no longer have barns and small wooden outbuildings but huge sheds for tractors and other equipment, and storage bins for grain. Dairy farms, cattle ranches, and other farms rely on large metal barns and shelters for livestock. Most of the old-time farms have long since vanished. So, too, have the people who worked them and their way of life. Now and then the simple outline of a barn can be seen rising from a field of corn or wheat. But most of these barns are empty now—ghosts of America's rural past.

GLOSSARY

adobe   sun-dried bricks made of clay and straw

adz   a sharp-bladed tool shaped like a hoe and used for smoothing the surface of timbers

auger   a hand tool used for drilling holes in wood

board and batten   barn sheathing of narrow vertical boards nailed over the cracks between wide boards

broadax   an ax with a short handle and wide blade used for squaring logs

cantilever   to project outward to form an overhang

clapboards   overlapping boards, often thicker on one edge than the other, placed horizontally to cover the outside walls of a building

dugout   a home made by digging a hole in a hillside and building a log or lumber front wall and roof

fodder   livestock feed, usually coarsely chopped grass or corn

forebay   an overhang on a barn, under which animals take shelter

gable   the top section of a wall under the point of a pitched roof; usually triangular

gambrel roof   a roof with two slopes on each side

haymow   a place for storing hay; also known as a hayloft

Homestead Act   a law passed by Congress in 1862 granting 160 acres of land to any person who agreed to live on and cultivate the land for five years

mortise-and-tenon   having slots and projecting parts that fit together to connect the ends of timbers

post-and-beam   a type of timber construction using vertical posts and horizontal beams

rafters   the boards or beams that form the roof structure of a building

rancho   a one-story, Spanish-style house often with a courtyard and a corral for livestock

shingles   the split wooden boards used to cover a roof

sod house   a small dwelling made by stacking layers of prairie turf; also called a soddy

thatch   straw or reeds used to cover a roof

treenail   a wooden peg that holds timbers together

51

FURTHER INFORMATION

BOOKS FOR YOUNG READERS

Bial, Raymond. *Frontier Home*. Boston: Houghton Mifflin, 1993.

Henry, Joanne Landers. *Log Cabin in the Woods: A True Story About a Pioneer Boy*. New York: Four Winds Press, 1988.

Patent, Dorothy Hinshaw. *Homesteading: Settling America's Heartland*. New York: Walker, 1998.

Sherrow, Victoria. *Huskings, Quiltings, and Barn Raisings: Work-Play Parties in Early America*. New York: Walker, 1992.

WEBSITES

ALHFAM, in particular, provides excellent links to the home pages of eighty excellent living history, agricultural, and open-air museums.

ALHFAM The Association for Living History, Farm and Agricultural Museums
http://www.alhfam.org/welcome.html

BARN AGAIN!
http://www.agriculture.com/ba/ba!home.html

The Dutch Barn Preservation Society
http://www.schist.org/dbps.htm

El Rancho de las Golondrinas
http://www.golondrinas.org/

Historic Farms
http://www.mtsu.edu/~then/HistFarms/

Garfield Farm and Inn Museum
http://www.garfieldfarm.org/

Hale Farm & Village
http://www.wrhs.org/sites/hale.htm

Living History Farms
http://www.ioweb.com/lhf/

The Preservation of Historic Barns
http://www.oldhouseweb.com/oldhouse/content/npsbriefs/brief20.asp

South Dakota State Agricultural Heritage Museum
http://www.agmuseum.com/

BIBLIOGRAPHY

Brownstone, Douglass L. *A Field Guide to America's History*. New York: Facts on File, 1984.

Endersby, Elric, Alexander Greenwood and David Larkin. *Barn: the Art of a Working Building*. Boston: Houghton Mifflin, 1992.

Harris, Bill. *Barns of America*. New York: Crescent Books, 1991.

Hawke, David Freeman. *Everyday Life in Early America*. New York: Harper & Row, 1988.

Howe, Nicholas S. *Barns*. New York: MetroBooks, 1996.

Noble, Allen G., and Hubert G. H. Wilhelm. *Barns of the Midwest*. Athens, OH: Ohio University Press, 1995.

Rawson, Richard. *The Old House Book of Barn Plans*. New York: Sterling Publishing Co., 1990.

Ridge, Martin. *Atlas of American Frontiers*. Chicago: Rand McNally, 1993.

Sloane, Eric. *Our Vanishing Landscape*. New York: W. Funk, 1955.

Time-Life Books. *The Pioneers*. New York: Time-Life Books, 1974.

Tunis, Edwin. *Colonial Living*. New York: Crowell, 1976.

Tunis, Edwin. *Frontier Living*. New York: Crowell, 1976.

INDEX

*Page numbers in **boldface** are illustrations*

Raymond Bial has published over fifty critically acclaimed books of non-fiction and fiction for children and adults. His photo essays for children include *Corn Belt Harvest, County Fair, Amish Home, Cajun Home, Frontier Home, Shaker Home, The Underground Railroad, Portrait of a Farm Family, With Needle and Thread: A Book About Quilts, Mist Over the Mountains: Appalachia and Its People, The Strength of These Arms: Life in the Slave Quarters, Where Lincoln Walked, One-Room School, A Handful of Dirt*, and *Ghost Towns of the American West*.

He has written Lifeways, a series published by Marshall Cavendish about Native Americans, traveling to tribal cultural centers, to photograph people, places, and objects that reflect the rich history and social life of Indian peoples.

Building America is the author's second series with Marshall Cavendish. As with his other work, Bial's love of social and cultural history and his deep feeling for his subjects is evident in both the text and the illustrations.

A full-time librarian at a small college in Champaign, Illinois, he lives with his wife and three children in nearby Urbana.